I Want A Bearded Dragon

2020 Edition

Tristan Pulsifer and

Jacquelyn Elnor Johnson

Crimson Hill
Books

www.CrimsonHillBooks.com

First edition, October 2016.

Revised, January 2020.

Cataloguing in Publication Data

Pulsifer, Tristan | Johnson, Jacquelyn Elnor

I Want A Bearded Dragon | Best Pets For Kids Series

Description: Crimson Hill Books trade paperback edition | Nova Scotia, Canada

ISBN 978-0-9953191-9-6 (Paperback)

BISAC: JNF003190 Juvenile Nonfiction: Animals - Reptiles & Amphibians |
JNF003170 Juvenile Nonfiction: Animals – Pets |
JNF051150 Juvenile Nonfiction: Science & Nature – Zoology

THEMA: YNNM - Children's / Teenage general interest: Reptiles & amphibians |
YNNH - Children's / Teenage general interest: Pets & pet care

Record available at https://www.bac-lac.gc.ca/eng/Pages/home.aspx

Cover Photo: Sannie32, Stockfresh.com
Book design: Jesse Johnson

We are pet owners, not veterinarians. Nothing included in this book is meant to serve as medical advice. If you suspect your pet is ill, please see your local vet. We accept no liability concerning your pet ownership.

Crimson Hill Books
(a division of)
Crimson Hill Products Inc.
Wolfville, Nova Scotia
Canada

Contents

<u>Introduction</u>

What is a Bearded Dragon?

A young bearded dragon resting on a rock in his tank. Beardies especially like having rounded rocks or branches to climb on.

A bearded dragon is one type of lizard. Wild bearded dragons live only in Australia.

Some very odd and unusual animals developed in Australia, but nowhere else. This happened many thousands of years ago.

Australia gave them their ideal place to live. Ideal means there is enough food and shelter and few natural enemies.

Some of these Australian animals are ones you may have seen in books, on TV or at the zoo. This includes kangaroos, koala bears and the oddest animal of all, the platypus.

But what do you know about another Australian native creature, the bearded dragon?

Bearded dragons are not really dragons. They can't breathe fire or fly like dragons do in stories.

But the first part of a bearded dragon's name is true. They do have a beard. It's not like a man's beard or a goat's beard.

It's not like any other beard in the world!

Bearded dragons are good at climbing.

They can also run fast. Some types of dragon lizard can even stand up and run on their hind legs!

Wild bearded dragons live in dry places, like deserts, but also where there are trees.

There are eight types of bearded dragon. Some live near the ocean. Others live inland. Pet beardies come from two types of inland bearded dragon.

This is a juvenile bearded dragon. A juvenile is older than a baby, but not an adult yet. (Juvenile people are sometimes called teenagers.)

Baby Beardies

In summer, female beardies make a shallow nest in sandy soil. They lay up to 16 eggs.

The babies are tiny when they first break out of their leathery eggs. They aren't much bigger than your middle finger.

Baby beardies eat A LOT. They grow quickly. Just 4 weeks after they hatch they are already 8 inches (or 20 centimeters) long!

Babies usually have an orange stripe near their eyes. This stripe fades as they get older.

This is a baby beardie.

By the time they are 18 months old or so, beardies are adults. This means they are ready to have their own babies.

Adults are 18 inches to 24 inches long (or 45 to 61 centimeters long). Usually, males are a bit bigger than females.

This might sound big to you, but half of their length is their tail.

Baby Tank

Beardie babies are fine in a smaller glass tank. But as they grow, they need more space! The tank needs to be three times as long as they are. For an adult, a tank that is 6 feet (2 metres) long is the right size.

Beardie Fun Fact

Can your bearded dragon see in colour? The answer is, "Yes!" Beardies can see every colour except red.

This is a pet leopard gecko. They're much smaller and usually more timid than a bearded dragon.

Is a bearded dragon like a leopard gecko?

In some ways bearded dragons and leopard geckos are alike.

They are both lizards. Like all lizards, their legs are on the sides of their bodies. Their eyes are on the sides of their heads.

Their heads are triangle-shaped.

The top side of their bodies are colourful. They have smooth bellies.

All lizards are reptiles.

There are just a few reptiles that enjoy being pets or living at a zoo.

Among lizards, leopard geckos and bearded dragons are considered to be the two best pet choices. They are gentle and friendly and can be happy as pets.

They are also easier to care for than most other pets that are reptiles.

The creatures in the reptile family look very different from each other. But they have some important things in common.

They all have scales. Their babies hatch from eggs. They spend most or all of their time on land. Some, including bearded dragons, can swim.

Except for birds, all reptiles are cold-blooded.

What does cold-blooded mean?

Cold-blooded means they must have sun to warm their bodies. They must find a cool place to rest when they get too hot.

Mammals are different. Dogs, cats, horses, bears, foxes, mice and people are all mammals.

All mammals are warm-blooded. This means they can use energy from their food to warm their bodies. They

Baby Lewie. Photo by D. Pulsifer.

can cool off by sweating when they get too hot. No reptile except birds can do this.

Mammal babies are born alive, not from eggs (except for a few unusual mammals, like ant-eaters and that oddball animal, the platypus).

Veggies and leafy greens are very good for beardies.
Photo by D. Pulsifer.

One of the friendliest, sweetest and most fun to know of all the creatures that can be a pet is the bearded dragon.

We're excited that you've joined us to find out more about them and just how cool and interesting beardies can be.

Chapter One

Why can a Bearded Dragon be a Good Pet?

This is Lewie. He's 6 months old. He enjoys basking in his tank.

Bearded dragons don't take up much space. They can't make any sound.

They have a friendly personality.

Most of them like to be with people. They are very curious. They love attention and they love to be petted.

Unlike some other pets, bearded dragons sleep at night. They are awake and active during the day, like people.

Though it is true that they can bite, they almost never do. They might bite when they think they are being hurt or attacked.

When they are adults, they eat mostly fruits and vegetables – the same ones people eat.

These are just some of the reasons beardies make great pets. They also have some really interesting abilities.

They have excellent hearing. They can hear you coming before they see you. Maybe they're hoping you're coming for a visit, or to give them something nice to eat.

Beardies have good eyesight, too. They can see in most colours, but not red.

They can also see in the dark far better than any human can. Humans don't have very good night-vision, but some animals do. Beardies are among the best at being able to see when there is hardly any light.

What would it look like to look through your beardie's eyes in the dark?

Imagine that one night you woke up and it was really, really dark out.

You decide not to turn on a light because suddenly, you have the ability to see everything. But the odd thing is, everything is gray. Light gray, or medium gray, or dark gray.

You can see clearly, but nothing is in colour.

If this happened, you would be able to see exactly the same way a bearded dragon can see at night!

Bearded dragons are easy to tame and don't take a lot of time to care for. The care they need is fast and easy once you have their new home set up right.

They are also easy to keep healthy. With good care, they can live a long time. Eight or ten years is average, but some beardies live until they are 15, or even older.

Who would NOT enjoy having a bearded dragon and why?

If you want a pet just to leave in its tank or cage and look at, a beardie is not for you. Beardies want and need to have some alone time, but they also want to be with people.

They like to hang out with you and do what you're doing.

They enjoy being outside with you on a sunny day and catching some rays.

Some people like to put a leash on them and take them for a walk!

They also like having a dip in a shallow pool. The pool water should be as warm as if you were swimming in it. For beardies, it can't be deeper than up to the top of your beardie's legs.

If you want a pet who will run around outside with you, a beardie won't be a good choice.

This is also true if you don't have much time for a pet. Or if you travel a lot and are hardly ever home.

Beardies do love car rides. But they aren't really very good travellers. Also, most airlines won't let them in the cabin with the people. They have to travel in a pet crate with the baggage.

If you aren't comfortable handling insects or having them in your house, you probably won't enjoy having a beardie for a pet.

Also, it can cost more money than it does for other pets to get your beardie. They need a glass tank for their home. The tank has to have all these things:

- *A heat lamp at top or above.*
- *An ultra-violet full spectrum (UV) light, hung next to the heat lamp.*
- *Rocks or a sturdy climbing branch to give your beardie comfortable places to bask.*
- *Places to hide and sleep.*

And you'll also need:

- *Thermometer to measure temperatures at the warmer, middle and cooler places in your beardie's home.*
- *Plates or shallow bowls for food and water.*
- *A meter to measure the humidity in the tank.*

Beardie babies are cute and hungry. REALLY hungry.
They eat a lot of live insects.

A basking place is a nice warm place right under their UV light. Without this light (and getting enough of it every day) a pet bearded dragon will die.

Remember, bearded dragons can live a really long time, for a pet. If you are age 10 right now, your beardie could still be alive when you are 20 or even 25 years old.

These are important questions to ask yourself before you get a pet.

Are you sure you will always want this pet?

Are you ready to promise that you will always give them very good care? Will they get enough attention, even when you don't feel like it?

Will you be a responsible pet parent?

A happy and healthy beardie.

Chapter Two

Questions and Answers about Bearded Dragons

This is a wild bearded dragon. You can easily see his beard.

Where do pet bearded dragons come from?

Bearded dragons live only in eastern Australia.

Back in 1960, the government there passed a law to protect their country's wildlife. It was no longer possible to take any animal out of Australia without permission. If you did this, you were breaking the law.

Someone did, sneaking some inland bearded dragons out of Australia. They took them to Europe.

No one knows who did this, or exactly when. Or how they got away with it.

They kept these stolen beardies and started to breed and sell them as pets.

Today, all pet beardies are captive-bred. This means they are not wild and never were.

Beardies that are pets today are all the great-great-great (and some more greats) grandchildren of the beardies that were stolen out of Australia.

Beardies who are bred to be pets live much longer than wild beardies. This is because they get better care.

Pet beardies are bred to have brighter colours and bolder patterns. But pet beardies still behave like their wild cousins do.

Wild beardies mostly live alone

They are very territorial (say it like this: tare-a-tor-ee-all). Territorial means wanting to own the area they live in. Many animals are territorial when they are wild.

It's like not wanting anyone else to be in your own back yard, because everything in it belongs to you.

When two wild bearded dragons happen to meet up, they will quickly decide who is the bigger, stronger animal.

The less strong, younger or smaller beardie needs to back away. If they don't, they risk being attacked.

Beardies won't attack any creature except each other, or a small creature they want to eat.

But beardies can get bite-y with their human if they feel they aren't getting enough attention and playtime, or if their tank is too small. Not having enough space causes stress for a bearded dragon.

Just like with people, stress causes bad behaviour.

This beardie is starting to shed his skin so he can grow larger. The old skin comes off in big chunks.

Is a bearded dragon really a dragon?

No. Beardies probably got the name of "dragon" because they do look something like a friendly dragon. But with really short legs.

Just like other lizards, beardies can't fly, or breathe fire, or do anything else that is magical.

Is a bearded dragon really a dinosaur?

No. Scientists now think that some dinosaurs were reptiles, or a lot like some modern reptiles. But they probably weren't lizards.

Scientists are experts who do science for their job. They investigate and do experiments to discover new facts about animals, plants, our world and the universe.

It now appears to be true that dinosaurs were not cold-blooded, like most reptiles.

Some scientists think dinosaurs weren't warm-blooded, like birds or mammals.

So what were they?

Recent research suggests that dinosaurs were something in between warm-blood and cold-blooded.

Their true nature remains a mystery. It's a mystery scientists are eager to solve.

Bearded dragons are not like the ancient dinosaurs.

The closest relatives to dinosaurs are crocodiles and birds.

This means that dinosaurs never really became extinct. They just changed a lot into some creatures alive today.

Are bearded dragons poisonous?

Yes, but their poison is mild and completely harmless to humans. It can't hurt you.

Wild beardies use it to stun their prey.

A juvenile beardie. Photo by J. Johnson.

Can bearded dragons change colour? What colours do they come in?

Wild bearded dragons are usually brownish.

When they are babies, most beardies are light cream and brown on their backs.

Their colour changes and they get stripes and patterns as they grow into adults. Their bellies are always white, like milk or vanilla ice cream.

Pet bearded dragons have been bred to have brighter colours and more interesting patterns.

If you go to a zoo or a reptile show, you may see beardies that are mostly orange, reddish-orange, reddish-brown or gold and brown.

These fancy beardies are called morphs. Morphs always cost more than plain brown beardies. Some people are willing to pay more money to have a really unusual-looking pet that no one else has.

You won't see them at your local pet store.

But you can see morphs at reptile shows. These are usually held every year in larger cities.

These shows give you a chance to see lots of different reptile pets up close. Pets and pet equipment are for sale at these shows.

Often, reptile shows let kids in for free!

Why is that beardie waving his arm or nodding his head?

Bearded dragons can't make any sound. But they can use body language!

Human body language is nodding your head, or smiling, or shaking hands, or waving good-bye.

Animals also use body language to communicate with each other. And some pets have learned to use their body language to communicate with people.

When two beardies meet, and one nods their head or waves a front paw at the other, it means, "Hello, I see you. I know you are bigger and stronger than me. I am just going to stay over here and not try to attack you. Please don't attack me. I'm harmless."

Show us your beard, little beardie!

The one part of all beardies, both wild and tame, that does sometimes change colour is their beards.

When a beardie is stressed or ready to attack an enemy, they will puff out the skin under their chin.

The spiky scales turn darker than the usual colour, usually brownish-black. It looks just like they have a big hairy beard. That's how they got their name.

An orange morph beardie's beard doesn't turn brown or black. It turns bright orange!

Can beardies swim?

Yes they can if they have to. But they don't like to.

Beardies aren't natural swimmers. They only swim if there is a flood and they have to swim to survive.

They do enjoy a bath, especially when they are shedding.

Beardies shed their skin every time they are ready to grow larger. For this reason, baby beardies shed more often than adults do.

Pet beardies rarely display their beard like this one is doing. Photo by User:Obolton, WikiCommons.

You can let your beardie take a dip in a shallow dish or in a kiddie pool outside in sunny weather. The water should never be deeper than the top of their legs.

In colder or cloudy weather, let your beardie have a dip indoors. It's something fun you can do together.

Be sure to never leave your pet alone when he or she is outside or having a swim. For their safety, you need to stay with them any time they are not in their tank.

Here's another safety tip. Never have your beardie outside in sunshine and in their glass tank. Sun on glass can get super-hot, making the tank far too hot for your beardie.

It would be like being inside a car on a really, really hot day with all the windows closed and no air-conditioning. Any person or animal inside that car would die from the heat if they weren't rescued.

Are bearded dragons smelly?

No, not if you keep their tank very clean. This is easy to do. Just take away any food they haven't eaten after half an hour or so.

Scoop the poop with a spoon and flush it once a day.

Give the tank a complete cleaning with a mild disinfectant cleaner once a week. You should wear cleaning gloves when you do this. You will probably need someone older to show you how to clean your beardie's home.

What can become really smelly is the crickets. If you buy too many for your beardie to eat and some of them die, they really stink!

When you have a pet that eats live food, you also have to look after your feeder creatures. For pet beardies, feeder creatures are insect worms and crickets.

A beardie with a piece of kale.

Is it safe to handle a bearded dragon?

Yes, if you always remember to wash your hands and arms up to your elbows carefully with warm water and soap before AND after you touch your bearded dragon.

The reason you must do this is that some lizards can pass salmonella to people. When people get salmonella, they get an illness that is like having the flu.

It is very unlikely you will get sick from your pet, but it is always smart to be safe now, not sorry later.

Just using hand sanitizer is not enough to protect you from getting salmonella. Another important reason to wash your hands before you touch your pet is that you don't want your pet to catch some germs from you!

How much time does it take to care for a pet beardie?

All pets need a feeding, cleaning and exercise or socializing routine.

Just like people, they like to know when there is going to be something good to eat, where they are going to rest and sleep when they're tired and when it's going to be playtime.

Like people, pets are happiest when there is a good routine.

It will probably only take a few minutes each day to feed your beardie and scoop the uneaten food and poop.

Your beardie will be unhappy if it doesn't get time and attention from you. Beardies are most content when they get an hour or so of playtime with their people each day.

They are also happiest when they can see people coming and going during the day and maybe stopping for a quick visit. They don't like it when their tank is stuck off in a corner and they never get any attention.

You also need to remember to take care of your feeder crickets and mealworms. This is easy to do and takes just a few minutes, but you have to do it <u>every</u> day.

Should I get two beardies so they can keep each other company?

Wild bearded dragons always live alone for almost all of their lives.

It usually isn't a good idea to have pet beardies together in the same tank. If one is bigger or older than the other, or they are two males, and sometimes also when they are two females, one could attack and seriously injure the other.

If you put baby beardies together, they will fight. Some of the babies could lose the tips of their tails or toes. A lost tail tip or toe tip won't grow back.

If you put a male and a female together, you might get baby beardies. This is good if this is what you want, but baby beardies are more work than older ones.

For one thing, they have to each have their own tank to stop them hurting each other. And they need to be fed several times a day. It is sometimes very difficult to get a new baby beardie to eat.

How much help will I need from my parents (or someone older)?

If you are a sensible and responsible person, you can do many of the care tasks for a pet bearded dragon, but probably not all of them. You will need some help from a parent or someone older.

Here are some of the things you will probably need help with:

- Buying and setting up the new home for your beardie.
- Being sure your tank works properly
- Buying your beardie and getting him or her home.
- Setting up your care routine for your beardie
- Starting your care routine for the feeder insects
- Buying more feeder insects (available at pet stores or online).

From left to right, these pets are a juvenile bearded dragon, an adult beardie and a Pomeranian puppy.

What if I already have a dog or a cat?

Your dog or cat might be interested in being friends with your new beardie. Or they might decide your beardie is something to chase. Or to eat.

Pets can learn how to get along with each other. But it's smart to be careful introducing your pets to each other.

Be patient when you are teaching your pets to get along with each other. Never leave your beardie alone with your other pets.

An active and happy beardie. Photo by D. Pulsifer.

You also need a screen top on your beardie's tank to protect your pet. Make sure it fits securely. This way, a curious cat or dog can't get into your beardie's tank.

Chapter Three

How and Where to Get Your Bearded Dragon

Juvenile beardie Lewie on his travel hammock. Like most beardies, he likes going for car rides.

There are three ways to get your new pet beardie. There are good things, but also not-so-good things about each way.

The 3 ways are buy your pet at a pet store, buy your pet from a reptile breeder or adopt your pet.

1. Buy your pet at a pet store

A pet store might have been the first place you saw a beardie and decided you really want one.

The big advantage of buying your beardie at a pet store is you can see the pet you are getting up close. You can be sure he or she is healthy.

The problem with getting your pet from a pet store is that's usually the most expensive way to get your pet and all the equipment they need.

Unless you go to a specialty pet store that only sells reptiles, the pet store staff might not know much about bearded dragons. They could give you the wrong information. Or not be able to answer your questions.

They might not have given beardies the best care at a general pet store because they just don't know how to.

2. Buy your pet from a reptile breeder

You can meet reptile breeders at reptile shows. These are like trade shows for people who are interested in reptile pets.

To find these shows, or to find a quality reptile breeder if you can't go to a reptile show, look online.

Just Google "reptile show" or "herp show" or "bearded dragon breeders."

Herp is the short word for "herpetology." Herpetology (Say it like this: HER-pet-tall-oh-gee) is the science of studying reptiles and amphibians.

You may also have a reptile pet owners' club in your city or town. Go to their meetings. Ask the other members where they got their pets. Can they recommend a reliable bearded dragon breeder?

Good pet breeders only sell healthy animals.

This way of getting your new pet takes more time and effort. But you will also know that you have chosen a healthy pet that has been well-cared for by people who know about bearded dragons.

Your pet and supplies might also cost less than at a pet store when you buy directly from a reptile pet breeder or online.

Both new and used tanks, lights and other pet equipment usually cost much less when you buy them online.

Beardie Fun Fact:

Beardies in camo? It's true!

Wild beardies are able to change their colour to be exactly the same as the soil they are sitting on. No one knows exactly how they are able to do this. They use their beardie camo to hide from enemies that might eat them.

3. Adopt your new pet

Sometimes, good pet owners find they have too many pets, or they can no longer care for them and decide to sell them.

Look at free ads online for your city, state or province. One place to look is Kijiji. Two others are CraigsList and Gumtree. This is often the least expensive way to get your pet and also the tank, lights and other equipment you'll need.

The danger is that you could be adopting a pet that is ill or has not gotten good care. If you do adopt a bearded dragon, the first thing you need to do is take him or her to a veterinarian (a pet doctor) for a complete health check-up.

Be sure to choose a vet who knows a lot about reptile care.

This is always a good idea, when you get a new pet. It gives you the chance to ask the vet any questions you have about how to give your beardie a long, healthy life.

What if I get a bearded dragon and decide I don't really want him any more? Can I just give him back? Or let him go outside?

No. Once you have given a pet a home, you cannot simply give him or her back. Or let them go in your backyard. They are pets, not wild creatures. They do not know how to survive in the wild.

As a pet owner, if you have a pet you no longer want or can't take care of, it is your responsibility to find your unwanted pet a good, loving new home. They deserve to live with people who can give them good care and a happy life.

How much do pet bearded dragons cost?

The cost to buy your pet bearded dragon and everything they need depends on a lot of things. This includes where you live, where you get your pet, how old they are, if you want to get a morph and how fancy your tank set-up is.

Beardies cost about $50 to $100 from pet stores in United States or Canada, with babies costing less than adults. It will cost $250 to $1,500 or more for a morph.

If you live in England, Scotland, Ireland or Wales, you will pay about £20 to £50 for your beardie at a pet store. In Australia or New Zealand, a pet bearded dragon will cost about $100 to $150 from a pet store. In Japan, the cost is equal to about $100 to $500.

The tank and everything you'll need if you buy it new from a pet store will cost about $350 to $500 in Canada or the U.S. You will pay much less for a used tank.

Beardies always try to climb up. Make sure your beardie doesn't fall! They could be hurt if they do.

Some pet owners make their own tank. This is also less expensive than buying a new tank.

Beardie Fun Fact:

Did your beardie lose a front tooth?

It's OK. Beardies' front teeth fall out and they grow new ones all the time. This will happen for all of your pet bearded dragon's life!

But it is only true for front teeth. If they lose a side tooth, it is gone forever.

Should you get a baby bearded dragon?

Baby beardies are really cute. But babies need more time and a lot more care than adult beardies.

For one thing, babies need to be fed several times a day. A baby beardie can easily eat 100 crickets in a week, or more!

You'll want to be sure you can afford £20 to £40 pounds per month (if you live in Great Britain), or $25 to $75 or more per month (in U.S., Canada, Australia or New Zealand) for a baby beardie's live food.

Their live food is most expensive when you buy from a local pet store. It is cheaper when you buy your feeder insects online.

Some pet owners decide to grow their own feeder insects because this is much cheaper. But it is also more work.

With good care, a baby bearded dragon will become an adult before he or she is 24 months old.

Adults eat mostly vegetables and fruits and a lot less insects than baby or juvenile beardies.

Although an adult is bigger than a baby beardie, it actually costs less to feed an adult.

Which bearded dragon should I choose?

Choose a pet that is active and has lots of personality.

Beardies have been called the "puppy dogs" of the lizard pet world and they are. If the beardie you want isn't as lively and friendly as a puppy, it is probably ill.

Or it hasn't had enough time and attention from people and hasn't learned to be a good pet. This could be a sign that this beardie has been neglected.

Be sure that the beardie you choose has bright eyes and is a good eater. The tank or cage should be very clean, with no old food or poop that hasn't been cleaned up.

If a beardie has sunken, dull eyes, or watery eyes, or ignores his or her food, or is skinny in the legs or tail, it is sick. Don't buy it.

Before you choose your beardie, you need to get his or her new home ready.

Protect Your Beardie!

Protect your beardie from burning their feet or belly! Don't use an under-tank heating pad or heat strips that attach to the sizes of the tank. Don't put heated rocks in the tank.

All of these are sold as being safe for reptiles. They are really designed for pet snakes but can easily injure a bearded dragon. All of the heat in your pet's new home needs to come from safe heat lamps. To be safe, make sure that your pet can't ever get close enough to touch the lamps.

<u>Chapter Four</u>

Getting Ready for Your New Pet

Here's Lewie relaxing in his tank. Beardies will always try to get as close as possible to their heat lamp. Make sure they can't get close enough to burn themselves!

It's best to have everything you need to welcome your bearded dragon to his or her new home. Test it to be sure everything is working before you bring your pet home.

You need a tank that is set up just the way bearded dragons like. You also need the food they like to eat.

What kind of food do bearded dragons eat?

There are some lizard pets that can eat cat food. Some can eat reptile pellets for a short time, but it is not good for them.

They can not eat the kinds of meat that people eat, like chicken, turkey, beef or pork. They must get live insects because this is what their bodies are designed to use. Anything else makes them sick.

If you need to get a pet sitter for your beardie while you go away for a vacation, adult beardies can get along for a brief time eating reptile pellets instead of live insects.

To be healthy, beardies must have live insects and salads.

Baby beardies eat almost entirely insects, with just a little salad snack now and then.

Adult beardies eat almost entirely fruits and vegetables, with just a little insect snack once a week or so.

The insects pet bearded dragons eat are crickets and insect worms. Insect worms are insects like beetles in the worm stage of their life cycle.

Protect your beardie!

You cannot feed your pet any insects you catch in a field or in your backyard.

When you're outside, don't let your beardie eat ladybugs, mosquitos, butterflies, moths, bees, wasps, centipedes or anything else that's out there.

Wild insects could be full of gardening or farm field chemicals like weed-killer. They might also have parasites.

Eating wild bugs could make your beardie very sick.

Never let a beardie eat a firefly. Even eating just one firefly can kill a bearded dragon!

Crickets

You can buy crickets in several sizes. You need the smallest size, the minis, to feed baby beardies.

This is because a little beardie could easily choke or have a problem digesting the food if it tries to swallow food that is too big.

Keep your crickets in a cricket pen or a plastic container with a tight lid. It needs a few small holes in it, so your crickets get some air to breathe. A clean food container works for your cricket home.

Cut up paper egg cartons and put the pieces into your cricket home. Crickets need hiding places. If they don't have them, they will go a bit crazy and start eating each other!

Feed your crickets apple, potato or carrot slices and raw oatmeal. Cricket water pillows (you can buy these online) make it easy to be sure your crickets get enough water. They will also live longer if they aren't thirsty.

Insect worms

There are several types of worms that beardies eat.

This includes waxworms, superworms and butterworms. Juveniles can have any of these types of worms as long as they are small enough.

These worms are loaded with protein and fat. This is exactly what young beardies need to grow strong. For adult beardies, worms are a treat, once or twice a week. Too many worms, and you will have a fat pet that isn't as healthy and won't live as long.

This is a hornworm, crawling on a piece of egg carton in a plastic container.

Each type of worm needs its own home. Set it up the same as your cricket home in a plastic container, with a lid with a few tiny holes for more air and cut up egg carton pieces. Feed insect worms the same things you feed your crickets, except when you gut-load them. They don't need cricket water.

Bearded dragons love insects, especially dubia roaches, grasshoppers and locusts. You can buy them from pet shops or online. Be sure to get the right size, because trying to eat an insect that is too large can make your beardie sick.

The right size for your beardie is a live insect that is no longer than the space between your pet's eyes. Never let your beardie eat insects you catch outside. Wild insects almost always have parasites. They could be poisonous for your beardie!

A yellow beardie morph about to catch a grasshopper.
Photo: Steve Greer, Flickr.

Gut-load your feeder insects

Gut-loading your feeder insects is one more thing you must do to keep your beardie healthy. Gut-loading means you give a superfood to the insects before you give those insects to your pet.

There are two ways to gut-load your feeder insects. You need to do both to help your beardie digest their food and have strong bones.

Beardie Fun Fact:

How long will your pet bearded dragon live? With good care, pet beardies live eight to 10 years but some can live until they are 14 or 15 years old.

Here's method one:

Mix all of these things in a blender or food processor: equal amounts of oatmeal, wheat bran, whole-grain flour, tropical fish food and rabbit food pellets. (You can buy all of these at the grocery store and pet store or online).

Feed this dry mixture to your feeder insects for the two days before you feed the insects to your beardie.

If you don't want to or can't make this dry mix, you can buy it already made up at some pet stores and online.

Here's method two:

Just before you feed insects to your beardie, place the insects in a small baggie or paper bag. Spoon in some bearded dragon supplement (you can buy this at the pet store or online).

Shake gently, so the insects are totally covered with the powder.

Make sure what you buy contains calcium, Vitamin D3 and reptile multi-vitamins. You won't get all of this in one product. Usually it's two. Give your beardie his or her powder-covered insects once a week.

Vegetables and Fruits

Give your beardie lots of green leafy vegetables in a shallow dish.

Tristan feeds kale to Lewie. Kale is a healthy leafy green vegetable.

Leafy green veggies are collard greens, bok choy, endive, basil, cilantro or mint leaves and kale. Break washed greens up into small pieces to make it easier to eat.

Beardies like dandelion leaves and the leaves, roots and flowers of clover plants. But don't just pick them from the side of the road. Roadside plants are full of car exhaust. This is poison for beardies.

They also like apples, berries, kiwi, winter squash and prickly pears. Remove the cores, stems, pits or seeds from fruits and veg and always cut it into small pieces.

Here are things you can NEVER feed your beardie.

Your beardie will get sick if you give them any of these:

- Avocado – this is a poison to bearded dragons
- Rhubarb
- Onions or garlic
- Mushrooms
- Canned fruits or vegetables
- Frozen fruits or vegetables
- Broccoli
- Cauliflower
- Beets
- Spinach
- Parsley
- Corn
- Potatoes

And they should also NEVER have:

- Head lettuce
- Romaine lettuce
- Watermelon
- Cucumbers

These four foods take more energy to digest than the food energy they give. That's why people on a weight-loss diet eat them – to get full without getting a lot of calories.

What kind of tank will my bearded dragon need?

The tank you choose for your bearded dragon needs to be glass. Some people choose plastic, but living in a plastic box isn't really healthy for a beardie.

They can't see out and you can't see in except from the top. And it also doesn't look very nice.

After all, when you have a pet you like, you want to see them. And they want to see you.

A smaller tank is fine for a baby beardie. But as they grow they need more space.

Your tank needs a secure screen lid. Beardies can't climb out of a glass tank, but you want to keep other pets away from your beardie.

There are several things you need inside a bearded dragon's tank.

Beardies must have heat from a heat lamp above the tank. This heat light needs to make it about 100 degrees F. (38 degrees C) on the warm side of their tank and allow it to be about 75 to 80 degrees F. (24 to 27 degrees C) on the cooler end of the tank.

Tank lights need to be on a timer that switches the lights on in the morning and off in the evening.

Beardies are like us. They're awake during the day and they want to sleep at night. They need darkness to be able to sleep, just like we do.

Your tank must have an Ultraviolet (or UV) lamp at the top of the tank. Wild beardies get all the UV rays they need from the sun.

That's why they bask. Basking is sitting on a branch or a rock and snoozing in the sun. Their bodies are collecting warmth and healthy UV rays. The UV rays give them natural vitamin D.

Pet beardies get the same healthy rays from basking under their UV light. It helps them digest their food.

Your tank needs a cooler side and a warmer side, so the beardie can go where it is most comfortable right now.

They also want places to hide, when they need some alone time. You can buy cool-looking hides at pet stores.

Or you could make your own out of a plant pot, a bowl...or? Get creative!

Just be sure your hides are big enough for your beardie to easily get into and out of. They must have no sharp edges.

Bearded dragons need a food dish and a water dish

Choose shallow dishes for food and water.

Never leave uneaten insects in the tank. If your beardie isn't hungry and falls asleep, crickets or insect worms could bite your beardie!

Also, don't give them tap water, unless your home uses well water. City and town water usually have fluoride, chlorine and other chemicals that are harmful for pets. Give them filtered water or spring water.

Beardies need places to climb!

Bearded dragons climb to get close to their sunshine or UV light. Their basking place needs to be about 12 inches (or 30.4 centimeters) away from the UV lamp.

Give your beardie some smooth, rounded rocks or a big climbing branch, or both. They enjoy a tank with lots of interesting things in it. It keeps them from being bored and is more like their natural world.

If you choose a climbing branch, make sure it did not come from an evergreen tree.

Cedar is poisonous to bearded dragons. Pine, hemlock and yew (these are other types of evergreen trees) could also make a beardie get sick.

Good choices for your pet's climbing branch would come from any of these types of trees:

- Oak
- Maple
- Aspen
- Dogwood
- Apple, cherry or any other fruit tree

Rocks that have been cleaned and disinfected, with no sharp edges, are safe.

If you put anything made out of plastic in the tank, make sure it is made out of non-toxic plastic (the same kind of plastic baby bottles are made from).

What else does a beardie need in his or her tank?

1. **Thermometers** so you can be sure the cool side and the warmer side are the temperatures beardies like. Do not use the stick-on type. They aren't accurate. You need the type that has a probe. Or use an infra-red gun thermometer.

2. At least two **places to hide** completely.

3. A **hygrometer**. This measures the humidity in the tank. Humidity is the amount of moisture in the air. If the air is too dry, or too wet, your beardie will get sick.

4. Possibly some **plastic plants**, if you like them. You could put in real plants, but make sure they are safe, such as ivy or herbs, because your beardie will eat them.

5. **Substrate** is what is on the floor of your beardie's enclosure. The best choices for a baby or juvenile are paper towel or newspaper, replaced daily. For an adult, you can use play sand. Get it at building supply stores.

This young beardie is too skinny. They need to be fed more crickets and insect worms.

What is substrate and why do I need it?

Substrate is what is on the floor of the tank.

You could use recycled paper or newspaper or paper towel that is shredded, but it doesn't look very nice. You have to change it every day.

Some pet owners use sand which is ok, but only for adults. Your baby beardie could accidentally swallow the sand. Babies and juveniles sometimes die because they eat sand.

You could not put in anything, but the smooth surface of the tank isn't really good for a beardie's feet.

Soil, bark, crushed gravel, mulch and crushed walnut shells are all bad for beardies. Don't use shredded cedar bark. It's poisonous for them!

A good choice is to buy a reptile tank mat. Get it at a pet store or online. These mats look something like fake grass. You wash them in hot water once a week.

The only danger is that your beardie might catch some bits of the cloth in their claws and try to eat the threads. Before the mat starts to fray, replace it to prevent this.

Where to put your bearded dragon's tank

Put your pet's tank in a place where you can enjoy seeing each other all the time.

It shouldn't be where there's a draft, right next to a room heater or in direct sunlight.

The tank also needs to be in a place that is dark and quiet at night and bright during the day.

Beardies must have heat and light. They will die without getting the right amounts of both.

Bringing your new bearded dragon home

Once you have your tank set up and you know it's working the way it should, it's time to get your beardie and bring them home!

Put them in a box with holes for air circulation and some shredded newspaper in the bottom.

If it is winter, warm up your car first. In summer, you might need some air conditioning.

Once you're home, put the opened box on its side in the tank. Let your new pet come out of the box when they are ready.

Give them food and water and leave them alone. Don't handle your new beardie for a week or so.

They need time to get used to their home and its sounds and smells.

Be patient about taming your bearded dragon. They need some time to get used to being a member of your family.

A healthy, alert beardie enjoying his brightly lit home. Photo: Milchdrink, Pixabay.com

What is Brumation?

If it is autumn or winter or the cooler season where you live and you have a sleepy beardie, don't worry. This is totally normal behaviour for adult bearded dragons.

What's happening is they're doing something like hibernating, only it's called brumation when lizards do it.

In the fall, they slow down and get doozy or want to sleep almost all the time. They might wake up long enough to get a drink of water, or to eat a little bit.

If your adult beardie seems to want to doze most of the time, don't try to wake them up by turning up the heat. They need their rest!

But you should watch them and weigh them once a week to be sure they aren't losing weight.

If they are losing weight, something else is going on and you probably need to take them to the vet!

Brumating dragons that aren't eating at all don't need their heat lamp on as long as the room they're in never gets colder than 70 degrees F. (21 degrees C.)

They also don't need their night heat lamp or their UV light on when brumating.

Brumation could last for 2 or 3 months. This is totally normal for beardies.

After that, gradually they'll wake up fully, be hungry, and need their lights back on.

Babies and juveniles don't go into brumation. Usually, the first time your pet will do this is after they're 1 year old.

Chapter Five

How to Tame Your Bearded Dragon

Be gentle when holding your beardie. Photo by J. Johnson

At first, just put your hand down in the tank. If your beardie comes over to say hello, or just to see if you have another delicious insect to give him, that's good. If he climbs onto your hand, he wants to come out to play. If not, try again later. Let your new pet get used to you slowly.

Beardies are curious. Sooner or later, your pet will be ready to make friends.

It could take a few weeks for your beardie to feel comfortable being touched and ready to trust you.

Be very gentle with your beardie!

You need to be kind and very gentle. Babies are especially delicate and easily hurt.

Never grab your beardie or squeeze him or her. Never pick him or her up by their tail.

Handle a beardie like you would a brand new baby kitten or puppy.

What could go wrong with your new pet?

Usually, very little can go wrong with a pet beardie.

They are easy to keep healthy and happy. They need all the things a healthy person must have. This is enough rest and sleep, a comfortable home, healthy food and water and loving attention.

A beardie that gets too fat needs to keep eating crickets but eat fewer worms. Use insect worms only for a treat, once a week.

A very skinny beardie that has no energy and won't eat is too hot, too cold or sick.

Check that both the cool side and warm side of their tank is the right temperature.

If they still have no energy, you might need to take your pet to a vet that knows about reptiles.

Sometimes pets will get along together but sometimes they won't. Always be careful when your beardie is out playing with other animals. It's no fun if someone gets hurt.

An adult bearded dragon in the wild.

What do beardies really like?

They like hanging out with you.

They like sitting on high places, like on your shoulder.

They like climbing onto your hand to let you know they want to visit with you.

They like their tank being changed around sometimes. Otherwise, they get bored.

They like warm baths and car rides.

They like having a chance to bask outside under the sun on a summer day.

They like greens and veggies.

They LOVE superworms!

What do beardies NOT like?

They don't like being picked up out of their tank. (They'd rather you wait until they climb onto your hand).

They are miserable if their tank is too small. Small tanks get too hot and there is no room to move around. A 10 gallon fish tank is too small!

Put the heat light and the UV light on timers that switch on at sunrise and switch off at sunset.

They can't eat if it is later than two hours until bedtime (lights out). That's because they need heat to digest their food.

If your home gets cooler than 65 degrees F. (18 degrees C) at night, you need a CHE heat lamp that is on a timer, so it turns on only at night. It won't create a light that keeps your beardie awake.

They don't like sharing their tank. It causes stress.

Photo: Harald Matern, Pixabay.com

These two dragons aren't just being friends. The beardie on top is showing dominance and also getting closer to the heat lamp. Dominance means telling the other animal, "I'm bigger and stronger than you are, so I get all the best things around here!"

The dominant beardie gets more food and the better basking spot in the tank. If you have a male and a female bearded dragon together, usually it will be the male who is dominant.

The danger is that your non-dominant pet will not get enough food or basking time. This will make them suffer stress and weaken them, making them more likely to get sick. This is why it is better to have one beardie per tank where they can't see each other.

Chapter Six

What to Name Your Beardie

Are you wondering what to name your new pet? If so, here are some ideas.

There are lots of books, movies and video games with dragons in them. You could choose one of their names.

Or maybe you don't want a dragon name, but you do want a name that starts with "B" (for beardie) or "D" (for dragon).

Or it could be a name that starts with the same letter as your name.

Or the name of your favourite candy, snack, ice cream flavour, car, actor, cartoon character, game or colour.

Here are some more name ideas for your pet beardie:

Sunny	Amber	Emerald
Slinky	Spyro	Sephora
Lizzy	Thor	Hercules
Leonides	Blade	Yoda
Bugs	Strider	Viper
Growler	Rex	Levi
Rocky	Google	Vampire
Ghost	Jordie	Nellie

Or how about these for a name?

Mushu (this was the dragon in the movie Mulan).

Puff (a magic dragon. There was a song about him).

Reptar (the green dragon in Rugrats).

Smaug (in The Hobbit).

Loki (the Viking god of mischief).

Blackbeard (a pirate).

Yeah. I'm awesome.

Why do bearded dragons have a beard?

When a bearded dragon is frightened or angry and ready to attack another creature, it will puff up this pouch of skin. Both the pouch and the scales turn a darker colour, usually brownish-black. It looks just like a scaly-beard.

The beard is meant to frighten their enemy away. It usually works!

Bearded dragons can be a wonderful pet!

This book doesn't tell you everything you (and your parents) need to know about bearded dragons.

Really, it's just the start of your new adventure as a pet owner...

If you are interested in reptiles and excited about getting one as a pet, you will want to read more about them.

This book has given a good idea of what it's really like to have a bearded dragon, and what you need to know to get started.

We hope you have a happy time getting to know your new pet beardie!

With good care, you two could be best friends for many years to come!

Best wishes,

Tristan and Jacquelyn

Got a question or comment?

Write to us here:

Jacquelyn@CrimsonHillBooks.com

A Few Final Words

Well here we are. You've come to the last page and now we're asking you for a kind favour.

Would you be willing to submit an honest review about this book and your experience reading it? You might need an adult to help you do this.

Your review could help someone else decide to give it a try.

Of course, we hope for a positive review, but most important is an honest one.

So, if you could take a few moments to help us and anyone who might be considering reading this book, thanks so much.

And warm best wishes,

Jackie, Wayne and Jesse

The team at CrimsonHillBooks.com

Crimson Hill
Books

More Fun Books For Kids Who Love Pets!

Best Pets for Kids series:

I Want A Leopard Gecko

I Want A Bearded Dragon

I Want A Puppy

I Want A Kitten

Fun Animal Facts for Kids series:

Fun Dog Facts For Kids 9-12

Fun Cat Facts For Kids 9-12

Fun Leopard Gecko and Bearded Dragon Facts For Kids 9-12

Fun Reptile Facts For Kids 9-12

Fun Pets for Kids series:

Small Fun Pets: Beginning Pets For Kids 9-12

Top 10 Fun Pets for Kids 9-12

Find them all at:
www.CrimsonHillBooks.com

Made in the USA
Las Vegas, NV
23 September 2023